WINSTON CHURCHILL SCHOOL
1300 W. 190th Street
Homewood, IL 60430

BUILDING A NATION

A NATION DIVIDED
1835-1900

Written by:
Stuart Kallen

A NATION DIVIDED

Published by Abdo & Daughters, 6535 Cecilia Circle, Edina, Minnesota 55439

Library bound edition distributed by Rockbottom Books, Pentagon Tower, P.O. Box 36036, Minneapolis, Minnesota 55435

Copyright© 1990 by Abdo Consulting Group, Inc., Pentagon Tower, P.O. Box 36036, Minneapolis, Minnesota 55435. International copyrights reserved in all countries. No part of this book may be reproduced in any form without written permission from the publisher. Printed in the United States.

Library of Congress Number: 90-082612   ISBN: 0-939179-90-3

Cover Illustrations by: Marlene Kallen
Inside Photos by: Bettmann Archive

Cover Illustrations by: Marlene Kallen
Edited by: Rosemary Wallner

TABLE OF CONTENTS

Chapter 1: The Mexican-American War 4
   Trouble in Texas
   Massacre at the Alamo
   Texas Joins the United States
   Trouble with Mexico
   War!

Chapter 2: Life in the 1850's 13
   New Inventions
   Life in the North
   Life in the South

Chapter 3: Slavery's Evil Grip 17
   The Life of a Slave
   The Slave's World
   Slave Rebellions
   The Underground Railroad
   The Abolitionists
   Uncle Tom's Cabin

Chapter 4: A Divided Nation 25
   Trouble in the Plains
   A New Man for a New Party
   The Union Divides

Chapter 5: The War Between the States 28
   Choosing Sides
   The Union's Position
   The Confederate's Position
   Who Will Fight?
   Blacks in the War
   A Deadlier Kind of War
   The Battle of Bull Run
   The War at Sea
   The War Rages On
   The Emancipation Proclamation
   Behind the Lines
   Women in the War

Chapter 6: The Beginning of the End 42
   Gettysburg
   Ulysses S. Grant
   Sherman's March to the Sea
   Reconstruction

Index 48

CHAPTER 1
THE MEXICAN-AMERICAN WAR

Trouble In Texas

By 1830, the United States was expanding its horizons by leaps and bounds. The vast, open lands of Texas attracted many Americans. The warm climate and empty spaces were perfect for ranching and growing cotton. By 1830, over 20,000 Americans lived in Texas. Only 4,000 Mexicans lived there at that time.

The lands of Texas were owned by Mexico. Slavery was illegal in Mexico. But many Americans that settled in Texas brought slaves with them to work in the cotton fields. The Americans refused to give up their slaves. Soon, the government of Mexico stopped letting Americans move into Texas.

In 1832, Antonio Lopez de Santa Anna became president of Mexico. Santa Anna made himself president for life, which enraged many Texans. Folk hero Davy Crockett organized a group of Tennessee militia men to help Texas fight for independence.

In 1835, Americans from all over Texas met in Austin to form an army. They elected Sam Houston as their leader and started training soldiers to fight for the Mexicans.

Davy Crockett.

Massacre at the Alamo

On March 2, 1836, Houston declared Texas to be an independent country. Forty-six men drew up the legal framework for the new country. While they were preparing the documents, 4,000 Mexicans were gathering at an old mission in San Antonio called the Alamo. Davy Crockett and Jim Bowie, were preparing for battle.

The Mexicans attacked the Alamo. For 13 days the Americans held back the force of 4,000 Mexicans. But the Texans were doomed. At the end of the battle, all 187 Texans lay dead.

When news of the Alamo reached other Americans in Texas, they demanded revenge. On April 21, Houston's army attacked Santa Anna's army in San Jacinto. The Texans decended on the Mexicans yelling, "Remember the Alamo!" Although greatly outnumbered, Houston's men took the Mexicans by surprise. Within 15 minutes, Houston's army had defeated the Mexicans.

Santa Anna fled the battlefield dressed in a private's uniform. Some Mexicans recognized him and saluted him. When he was identified by the Mexicans, Santa Anna was captured by Houston.

The Battle at the Alamo.

By threating him with the hangman's rope, Houston forced Santa Anna to sign a peace treaty granting Texas independence. The treaty made the Rio Grande River the southern border of Texas.

Texas Joins the United States

Texas remained an independent country after it signed the peace treaty with Mexico. The president of Texas, Sam Houston, encouraged thousands of Americans to move to Texas. He even offered free land to new settlers. Most of the people that moved to Texas were white southerners who used slaves to grow cotton.

Texans wanted to become part of the United States and asked Congress to make Texas a state. Many people in the United States did not want Texas to become a state because they did not want another state where slavery was legal. Also, Mexico still claimed portions of Texas. If Texas became part of the United States, Mexico would declare war. Despite the fear of war, in 1845 Texas became the 28th state to join the union.

Trouble with Mexico

When Texas became a state there was immediate trouble with Mexico. The United States claimed that the Mexican-Texas border was the Rio Grande River. Mexico claimed that the border was 200 miles north at the Nueces River. The area in between the Rio Grande and Nueces rivers was settled by Mexicans.

General Sam Houston

In February 1846, President James Polk ordered General Zachary Taylor to move troops to the Rio Grande. Taylor's troops reached the Rio Grande on March 28. Small towns in the area had been abandoned. The Mexicans that lived there had fled when they saw the approaching columns of men with guns and cannons. Taylor built a fort on the Rio Grande. The Mexicans across the Rio Grande stared in wonder at the sight of a large army on the banks of a peaceful river.

President Polk knew that moving the army to the Rio Grande would provoke the Mexicans to battle. On April 25, sixteen of Taylor's men were ambushed and killed by Mexicans. Taylor ordered that 5,000 volunteers from Texas and Louisiana join his army. Taylor sent a message to Polk that said, "Hostilities may now be considered as commenced."

Some Americans opposed the war. Many big city newspapers tried to make the war look glorious and its soldiers heroic. Poor men were dragged from their homes to join the army. Many times, they had no money to leave their wives and families. But volunteers were hard to find. Anyone bringing in acceptable recruits was paid two dollars a head.

War!

By early 1847, the American army was pushing deep into Mexico. Colonel Stephen Kearny took over New Mexico and California. (Both were Mexican possessions.) The Mexicans outnumbered the Americans in every battle, but the Americans had better weapons. In most battles, twice as many Mexicans died as Americans.

During the war, most American soldiers did not die in battle. They died from disease. Two-thirds of the army tents were old and rotten. When rain fell for weeks at a time, many soldiers got sick and died. Other places in Mexico were unbearably hot. Men were forced to march for months to get to battlegrounds. The water was so impure that thousands of soldiers died from drinking it. The food, which was often bad, also killed many men.

As tens of thousands of people on both sides died, the war raged on. Soldiers on both sides deserted their armies. American officers were often faced with mutiny from tired, angry soldiers. Officers whipped or hung deserters.

Finally on February 2, 1848, Mexico surrendered to the United States. The United States now owned the land that would become Texas, New Mexico, Arizona, California, Nevada, and Utah.

The price of victory was 13,000 dead Americans. Only 2,000 had died in battle, the rest had died from disease or wounds. After the war, Mexican soldiers raged through their own villages, killing anyone who had helped the Americans.

CHAPTER 2
LIFE IN THE 1850'S

New Inventions

America in the 1850's was a thriving, booming country. New inventions were changing the face of America. In 1830, a stagecoach trip from New York to St. Louis had taken three weeks. In 1850, the same trip by railroad took only two days!

There was a revolution in communications. In 1837, Samuel Morse invented the telegraph. When it was put to use in 1844, information could be transmitted by a code of clicking sounds sent through wires. Before the telegraph, news took weeks to travel across the country. By 1861, over 50,000 miles of telegraph wire transmitted news instantly. The Associated Press was founded in 1848. This was a news service that used the telegraph to send news to 3,000 newspapers all over the country. Americans, wherever they lived, could now read the same news at the same time.

In 1839, Charles Goodyear developed a process to vulcanize rubber. This process enabled rubber to withstand extremes of heat and cold. Vulcanized rubber allowed heavy duty drive belts to run machines.

Iron was needed to make machinery. Before the 1840's, wooden charcoal was burned to make iron. But the quality of the iron was poor. In 1840, the iron mills in Pittsburgh switched to anthracite coal for fuel. Thousands of people moved to Pennsylvania and West Virginia to become coal miners.

Life in the North
Many differences divided the northern states from the southern states. The North was a land of factories and businesses. Most people lived in large cities like New York and Boston. The Great Lakes region had growing cities like Chicago, Cleveland, and Buffalo. Oil, steel, farm machinery, and meat packing were the major industries. Almost all of the factories in the country were in the North.

Millions of unskilled laborers, many newly arrived from Europe, worked in the factories. Most of these people lived in dirty, overcrowded sections of large cities. About three-fourths of these immigrants came from Ireland and Germany. Blacks in the North were treated badly. They were not used as slaves, but they did not have equal rights. Prejudice against blacks was common.

Politically, wealthy businessmen from the North controlled the Congress and Senate. Most Northerners were against slavery and wanted it abolished (stopped). In general, the Northerners and the Southerners disliked each other.

Life in the South

The South was a region of farms and plantations. Cotton, tobacco, rice, and sugar grew well in the hot, wet climate. The few factories in the South manufactured goods from cotton or tobacco. Cotton and tobacco planters needed large numbers of slaves to work their land. In many places in the South, the population of black slaves outnumbered white people two to one. By the 1850's, the South was one of the few places in the world that used humans as slaves.

Most of the white population in the South were people whose ancestors had come from England or Scotland. Many Southern families had been in America for generations.

About 75 percent of the white people in the South were small farmers who owned a few slaves.

About 10 percent were poor white people who lived in backwoods cabins. About 15 percent of the white Southerners were wealthy planters who lived like kings on huge estates. Slaves made up about one-third of the population in the South.

A cotton plantation in the South.

CHAPTER 3
SLAVERY'S EVIL GRIP

The Life of a Slave

By 1840, almost 4 million slaves lived in the South. Slave owners treated their slaves like property. In town squares throughout the South, auctions were held every week. At these auctions, men, women, and children were bought and sold. Slave owners did not believe in slave marriages or families. Babies could be sold from their mothers' arms. Husbands could be sold to a planter hundreds of miles away from their wives. Many never saw their families again.

Some slaves were skilled laborers like blacksmiths, carpenters, and shoemakers. Some slaves worked as maids, nannies, and butlers for their masters. Most slaves worked as laborers, planting and harvesting crops. Slaves were forced to work from sunrise to sunset in the hot sun and pouring rain. In the winter, slaves would get frostbite because of the ragged clothes they were forced to wear. Most of the slaves were housed in broken-down shacks and were only fed scrap meat and corn.

Slave gangs were run by an overseer. Sometimes the overseer would whip or kill a slave who disobeyed his orders. Physical punishment was used to make slaves work hard for no reward.

The Slave's World
On plantations where slave families were allowed to stay together, family life was very important. Slaves that were sold to new owners often ran away to rejoin their families. On some plantations, slaves were allowed to use their free time to hunt and tend their own gardens.

Religion was an important part of a slave's life. Most slaves were introduced to Christianity by their masters. In general, slave owners made sure that the sermons the slaves heard talked about obedience and meekness. But slaves also used Christianity to hold their community together. Slaves stressed the importance of family, love, and kindness. Slaves used Christian spirituals to sing about Jesus and to protest slavery. Many slaves practiced a combination of Christianity and African religions and beliefs.

Many slaves were forced to put on a happy face to keep them from punishment. But while pretending to be happy, they would secretly break tools, slow down work, steal food, and pretend sickness. This was the only way that they could protest their conditions.

Escape was another reaction to slavery. But the chances of success were slim. Slaves were tracked with dogs as they traveled through unfamiliar countryside. When caught, they were bitten by dogs, whipped, or forced into difficult, dangerous labor. Despite these hardships, about 1,000 slaves escaped every year.

Slave Rebellions

One of the greatest fears held by southern whites was that their slaves would one day revolt. In 1831, Nat Turner, a slave preacher, gathered 70 men together. Inspired by a vision of black and white angels fighting, he led the men on a rampage, killing about 60 whites. The state militia responded by killing hundreds of blacks who had nothing to do with Turner. Turner and 18 others were captured and executed.

Turner's Rebellion sent shock waves through the South. Slave-owning politicians enacted harsh new laws restricting the actions of blacks. Free blacks were affected as well as slaves. The tougher codes made slavery even harder to resist.

Some people in the north were shocked as treatment of blacks became even worse. Many people felt that violence was the only answer to ending slavery.

The Underground Railroad
The Underground Railroad was not really a railroad. It was a network of black and white people who helped slaves escape to Canada where they would be free. These men and women led slaves along backcountry roads in the dead of night. During the day, slaves were hidden in barns, basements, or attics, far from the bloodhounds that where tracking them. Slaves were given food and clothing on the Underground Railroad. Night after night, the runaway slaves continued their journey until they reached freedom.

One of the most famous conductors on the Underground Railroad was Harriet Tubman. Tubman was a former slave who escaped to the North in 1849. After her escape, Tubman helped 300 slaves find freedom in the North. For 15 years Tubman risked her life night after night in the struggle against slavery. Slave owners offered a $40,000 reward for her capture. Tubman wore disguises and carried a pistol. She told her fugitives, "You'll be free or die. There is two things I have a right to, liberty or death. If I could not have one, I would rather have the other. For no man shall take me alive." Tubman helped slaves escape on the Underground Railroad until after the Civil War. After the war, Tubman traveled the country speaking out for equal rights for blacks.

Harriet Tubman (far left) photographed with a group of slaves whose escape she assisted. Harriet Tubman was a leader of the Underground Railroad.

The Abolitionists

People who were against slavery and wanted it abolished were called *abolitionists*. William Lloyd Garrison, a young printer in Boston, was one of the first white abolitionists. Garrison started a newspaper called the *Liberator*. In the paper, he wrote of the horrors of slavery and called for its immediate end. Garrison also started a group called the American Anti-Slavery Society. Members of this group talked at churches and town meetings. Many members of the society were former slaves.

Unfortunately, Garrison received little support for his position. Southern post offices refused to deliver abolitionist newspapers. Because Garrison verbally attacked Southerners, the state of Georgia offered a $5,000 reward to anyone who brought him to trial.

In the North, many people did not like slavery. But most did not want free blacks living in their communities. Many Northern whites feared that the blacks would take away their jobs. When abolitionists spoke throughout the North, they were often booed by audiences. In 1835, a Boston mob dragged Garrison through the streets. The police then threw him in jail! An abolitionist in Illinois was killed by a mob in 1837.

Fredrick Douglass was a former slave who was a member of the Anti-Slavery Society. Douglass had escaped from a Maryland plantation in 1838. He had taught himself to read and write. In the 1840's, Douglass lectured about the evils of slavery in England and America. He also published a newspaper called the *North Star*. He chose that name because the North Star helped slaves find their way north to freedom.

Uncle Tom's Cabin

Harriet Beecher Stowe was an abolitionist from Cincinnati, Ohio. One day she heard a story about a slave named Eliza. One winter, Eliza and her baby escaped from a farm in Kentucky. Eliza's journey to freedom brought her north to the Ohio River. The river was only partially frozen and she could not cross. Eliza and her baby waited through the cold winter night for the river to freeze.

The next morning, Eliza saw slave catchers and bloodhounds coming for her. Eliza wrapped her baby around her in a shawl and jumped. From one iceberg to the next, Eliza lept across the icy, flowing water. In time, Eliza made her way to Canada. The following summer, she returned to

Kentucky and helped her five children escape to freedom.

When Harriet Beecher Stowe heard Eliza's story, she decided to write a book about slavery and include Eliza's heroic journey. Stowe titled the book *Uncle Tom's Cabin*. When it was published in 1851, it became an instant best-seller. No book had ever sold as fast. *Uncle Tom's Cabin* helped many people in the North see the evils of slavery for the first time. More and more people became abolitionists.

Harriet Beecher Stowe, author of Uncle Tom's Cabin.

CHAPTER 4
A DIVIDED NATION

Trouble in the Plains

In 1854, the debate over slavery once again burst into the nation's capital. That year, Congress opened the Nebraska and Kansas territories to settlement. Senator Stephan Douglas suggested that the people in the territories decide for themselves whether or not they wanted slavery.

The people of Nebraska chose to enter the Union as a free state. Kansas could not decide. Northerners and Southerners rushed to Kansas, both sides hoping to influence the people there. Southerners wanted Kansas to be a slave state. Northerners wanted Kansas to be a free state. Suddenly, Kansas became an armed camp. Groups of men with rifles and guns rode through the countryside attacking the other side's towns. In all, 200 people were killed in the fighting.

A New Man for a New Party

While fighting was going on in Kansas, a new political party was forming in Wisconsin. The party was called the Republican Party. The Republicans took a strong stand against slavery.

They urged Congress to make slavery illegal. One of the new Republicans was a lawyer named Abraham Lincoln.

Lincoln was afraid that America would become two countries because of slavery. Lincoln said that a Union divided could not stand. All across the country, Lincoln made a name for himself as he gave fiery speeches about the Union. He was not opposed to slavery as much as he was opposed to the Union splitting up. Lincoln's popularity grew. In 1860, Lincoln was elected the 16th president of the United States.

Abraham Lincoln, 16th President.

The Union Divides

When Lincoln was elected president, Southerners decided they wanted to form their own country. They wanted to secede, or withdraw, from the Union. On December 20, 1860, South Carolina became the first state to secede from the Union. By February 1861, Mississippi, Georgia, Florida, Texas, Louisiana, and Alabama had seceded, also.

On February 4, 1861, representatives from the seven states met in Montgomery, Alabama. They named their new country the Confederate States of America. It was also called the Confederacy. People who lived there were called Confederates. The Confederates elected Jefferson Davis as their president.

On April 12, 1861, Confederate soldiers attacked Union soldiers at Fort Sumter, South Carolina. The Civil War had begun.

CHAPTER 5
THE WAR BETWEEN THE STATES

Choosing Sides

War fever swept the nation after the attack on Fort Sumter. On both sides, men were eager to begin the fight. Wives, sweethearts, and children cheered as soldiers marched down the streets of their towns. Most Americans thought the conflict would be over in a few weeks. No one was prepared for the horrible realities of war.

Because the Civil War was fought between two regions of the country, choosing sides was very difficult for some people. Family members and friends sometimes faced each other in battle. Abraham Lincoln's family was one of the divided families. His wife, Mary Todd Lincoln, had three brothers. All three sided with the Confederacy. Lincoln asked General Robert E. Lee to head the Union Army. Lee decided to command the Confederate Army instead.

Choosing sides was especially hard for those who lived in the border states. There were eight states that lay between the North and the South. They all allowed slavery but had close ties to the North.

Four states, North Carolina, Tennessee, Arkansas, and Virginia joined the South. Delaware, Missouri, and Kentucky stayed in the Union. People in northern Virginia did not want to fight with the Confederacy, so they formed their own state, West Virginia.

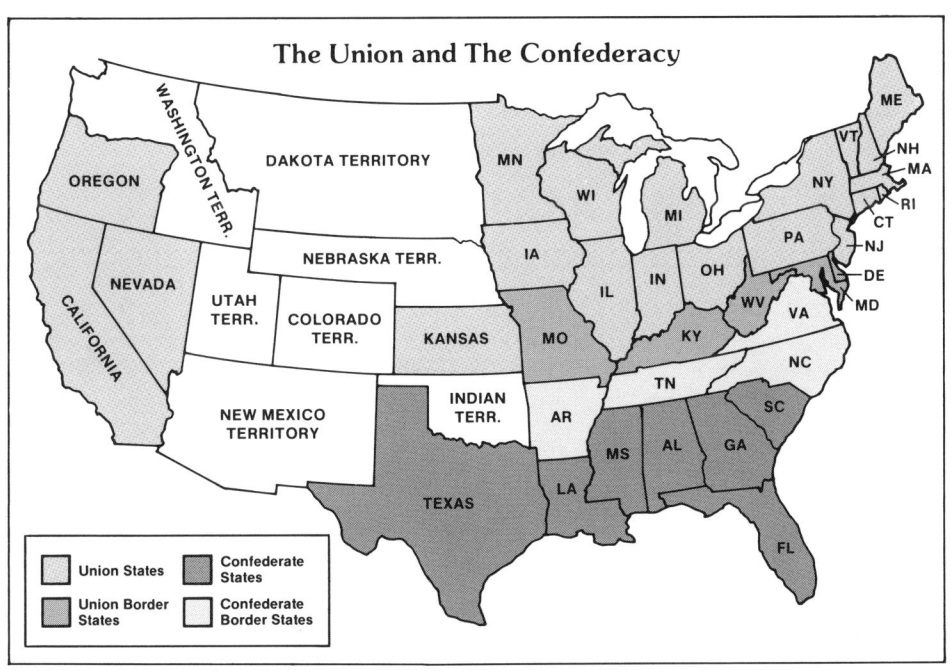

The state of Maryland was a problem for Lincoln. Maryland completely surrounded the nation's capital, Washington, D.C. Maryland however, wanted to join the Confederacy. Lincoln decided to jail anyone, including politicians, who were against the war. Lincoln jailed at least 15,000

29

people who committed no crime other than speaking against the Union. These people were not given a trial. Many of them were held in prison throughout the war. With many of its politicians in jail, Maryland finally sided with the Union. Throughout the war, there were many people in Maryland who worked as spies for the Confederacy.

The Union's Position
When the Civil War began, the Union had 22 states. The North had 22 million people while the South had only 9 million. The North had almost all of the factories. The states of Massachusetts alone produced more goods than the entire Confederacy. The North had most of the railroads and control of the Navy.

The Confederate's Position
When the war began, the South was confident of victory. They had no plans to invade the North. Their aim was to defend their homeland. Soldiers from the South were more experienced in the use of firearms and horses. The Confederacy also had the best military leaders in the country. Men like Robert E. Lee, Stonewall Jackson, and others had attended the United States Military Academy in West Point, New York.

General Thomas "Stonewall" Jackson, Confederate General.

Who Will Fight?

At the beginning of the war, both sides hoped to fill their armies with volunteers. Most people did not want to volunteer, so the Union Army tried to encourage people to join by offering a bounty. (A bounty is a sum of money paid to a man who joins the army.) Some men became bounty jumpers. They would join the army in one town, collect a bounty, then sneak off to another town to do the same thing. In this way, some men got rich.

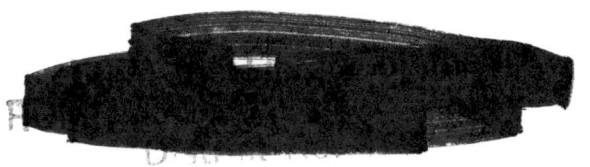

To build up their ranks, the Confederacy passed a draft law in 1862. The Confederate law stated that any man who owned 20 or more slaves would not have to fight.

In 1863, the United States passed its draft law. This law stated that all men between the ages of 18 and 45 were required to serve in the army. If a person had money, they could pay $300 to avoid serving.

People on both sides thought the draft laws were unfair because some men didn't have to fight if they had money or slaves. Because of this, people started saying that the Civil War was "a rich man's war and a poor man's fight." At least 10,000 boys ages 13 to 17 served in the war. One boy went into battle at age 9.

Blacks in the War

Even though the Union was desperate for soldiers, blacks were not allowed to join the army until 1863. Many blacks worked as cooks, drivers, and scouts for the army until then. Once they were allowed to join, blacks suffered harsh discrimination in the army. Blacks were often

given the most dirty and dangerous jobs. They received worse medical care than the whites. The weapons they were given were usually ones that had been thrown away by the white soldiers. White soldiers were paid $13 a month, black soldiers were only paid $10. Thousands of blacks fought for the Confederacy too, but most of them were forced to fight as slaves.

Company E colored infantry at Fort Lincoln - 1865.

Despite the hardships and discrimination, thousands of blacks fought bravely in the Civil War. In 1863, the all-black 54th Massachusetts Regiment led an assault on Fort Wagner in South Carolina. Nearly 100 black soldiers dodged gunfire and cannon fire to force their way into the fort. Once inside, the men engaged the Confederate soldiers in hand to hand combat. This display of courage won black soldiers some acceptance.

All in all, about 200,000 blacks fought for the Union. Many historians believe that the Union would have lost the war if it had not been for the skill and bravery of the black soldiers.

A Deadlier Kind of War
As both sides prepared for war, neither side realized how long and destructive the war would be. The North thought that once they captured the Confederate capital in Richmond, Virginia, the South would surrender. The South thought that if they pushed back several invasions by the Union Army, the North would give up.

During the Civil War, huge numbers of men faced each other for the first time in American history.

During the Mexican-American war, the largest battles had had about 15,000 soldiers opposing each other. During the Civil War, many of the battles had involved 100,000 men.

New inventions made the Civil War more deadly than other wars. Old style rifle balls were replaced by cone-shaped bullets which were twice as accurate. The Union manufactured cannons that could shoot a 300-pound cannonball. Sometimes these cannons were loaded with nails and chains. These weapons were extremely deadly.

Medical help was practically unknown on the battlefield. There were few doctors and water was often contaminated. The only painkiller was morphine, an addictive drug. Wounds were generally treated by cutting off the injured area with a saw. Arms and legs were piled up outside the medical tent as the screams of the wounded rose above the sound of gunfire.

The Battle of Bull Run
The morning of July 21, 1861, was a beautiful summer day. On this lovely morning, Northern picnickers and sightseers spread their blankets on a hill in northern Virginia, near Washington, D.C.

The hill overlooked a stream called Bull Run where the first battle of the Civil War was about to be fought. The picnickers thought that the brave Union Army would defeat the Confederacy and the war would be over in time for dinner. They were very wrong. Soldiers on both sides were poorly prepared for battle. At first, the Union troops fought bravely, but their advance was blocked by Confederate General Thomas Jackson. Jackson stood like a "stone wall." This earned the general the nickname Stonewall Jackson. Soon the Union soldiers threw down their guns and ran from the battlefield.

When the Union soldiers ran from the battlefield, their way was blocked by the frightened picnickers. Rushing to get away, the sightseers overturned their wagons and carriages. Horses fell as people ran for their lives. The road back to Washington was blocked for hours. The victory of the Confederate Army shocked the Northerners. For the first time, people realized that this war was not a game and that it would drag on for years.

The War at Sea

Before the war, the South had depended on the North and Europe for most of its manufactured goods. When the war began, the North stopped shipping goods to the south. More than ever, Europeans were needed for goods and supplies. The South sent many of its ships to Eurpoe for supplies.

After the defeat at Bull Run, Lincoln ordered the U.S. Navy to blockade the southern coast of the Confederacy from Norfolk, Virginia, to Galveston, Texas. Any ships bound for the South would be turned away by the Navy.

The plan worked. Before the blockade, 6,000 ships a year entered southern ports. During the first year of the blockade only 800 ships were able to make it through. As the war continued, the South began to run out of guns, ammunition, medicine, and other supplies because of the blockade.

The War Rages On

By September 1862, the South appeared to be winning the war. Confederate General Robert E. Lee had scored several victories over Union General George McClellen. The Union Army was defeated several times trying to take Richmond, Virginia. At a second battle of Bull Run, the Union was routed again. On September 17, at Antietam, Maryland, Lee won again. This day was the bloodiest single day of the war. Lee lost 11,000 men; McClellen lost 13,000.

The Emancipation Proclamation
President Lincoln said he was fighting the war to preserve the Union, not free the slaves. "If I could save the Union without freeing any slaves, I would do it," said Lincoln in August 1862. "If I could save it by freeing all the slaves I would do it; and if I could save it by freeing some and leaving others alone I would also do that."

As the war continued, abolitionists pressured Lincoln to free the slaves. On January 1, 1863, Lincoln issued the Emancipation Proclamation. (emancipate means to free.) The Emancipation Proclamation declared that all slaves in the Confederate states were free. The proclamation did not apply to any slaves behind Union lines. Therefore, Lincoln freed the slaves in Confederate states where he did not really have the power to do so. But he did not free the slaves in the Union where he did have the power.

Despite this logic, the Emancipation Proclamation set the wheels in motion for equal right for blacks. In some places in the North blacks were not allowed to attend school or vote. They were not allowed on public transportation. Suddenly, many Americans wanted equal rights for blacks in the North and South. A petition with 400,000 signatures asking for the end of slavery was sent to Congress in 1864. On January 1865, the 13th Amendment to the Constitution was adopted, ending slavery in America forever.

Behind the Lines

Soldiers weren't the only ones affected by the war. People were needed to grow crops, manufacture weapons, run the trains, and nurse the wounded. Many Northerners openly supported the Confederacy and were against blacks. In 1863 in New York City, a black orphanage was burned and many blacks were killed in the streets.

Some large industries in the North tripled their profits making goods for the war. Farmers grew record amounts of grain to feed the troops. Prices for goods, however, rose more than 50 percent, causing hardships for most people.

During the war, life in the South was filled with sorrow and hunger. Most of the fighting took place in the South. Farms and villages were reduced to burned rubble. Farm fields became bloody graveyards.

Because of the naval blockade, people had to do without items such as new clothes. Trains broke down and could not be repaired without parts from the North. Food could not be moved without trains. In cities like Richmond, people starved to death. Confederate money became worthless and prices skyrocked. In 1863, boots cost $250, coats cost $350. Two chickens cost $30, butter was $15 a pound. By the end of the war, flour sold for $1,000 a barrel. And this was when a Confederate soldier was being paid only $15 a month!

Women in the War
Although women were not allowed in the army, over 400 women dressed like men and fought in the Civil War. Besides fighting, women did all the necessary work needed to keep farms and cities running. Besides the work of raising children, women planted and harvested crops, manufactured equipment and clothing, and did many other important jobs.

Nursing became an important activity for women. At first, working in bloody hospitals and taking care of dying men was not considered proper work for women. But as the casualties piled up, women stepped in to help. The scenes these women faced every day were filled with horror and grief.

Clara Barton was a nurse who served in some of the bloodiest battles of the war. Later, Barton started the Red Cross. Many black women made a name for themselves during the Civil War. Sojourner Truth, an escaped slave, spoke out for equal rights for blacks and women. Charlotte Forten and Mary Peake taught former slaves to read and write. Harriet Tubman acted as a Union spy. Susie King Taylor, another escaped slave, was a nurse and teacher who later wrote about her experiences during the war.

Clara Barton.

CHAPTER 6
THE BEGINNING OF THE END

Gettysburg

As the year 1863 started, the bloody war dragged on. The Confederate Army had scored victories at Fredericksburg and at Chancellorville, Virginia. Still, the Union fought on. Robert E. Lee decided to invade Union territory to frighten the Northerners into surrender. This was the beginning of the end for the South.

On July 1, Lee's troops attacked Union soldiers at Gettysburg, Pennsylvania. For three days, 15,000 Confederates tried to break through the Union lines. When the clouds of gunsmoke finally cleared, thousands of Confederate soldiers lay dead or wounded. Lee had lost one-third of his men. Union losses were just as heavy, but Lee was forced to retreat to Virginia.

Ulysses S. Grant

Just as the battle of Gettysburg was ending, Union General Ulysses S. Grant was defeating the Confederate Army at Vicksburg, Mississippi.

On July 9, two black regiments beat the Confederates at Port Hudson, Mississippi. The Union now had control of the Mississippi River. Time was running out for the South.

Ulysses S. Grant.

Early in 1864, Lincoln made Grant commander of the Union Army. Grant devised a plan to defeat the South once and for all. Grant would move his army east to Richmond, Virginia. At the same time, General William T. Sherman would attack Atlanta, Georgia. The two generals planned to destroy the South. Not only would they fight all Confederate soldiers, but they would also kill anyone in their way.

Sherman's March to the Sea
On May 6, 1864, General Sherman and 100,000 soldiers left Chattanooga, Tennessee, for Savannah, Georgia. As the Union Army marched across Georgia, they lived off the land and left destruction behind. Sherman said of the march, "We have devoured the land and our animals eat up the wheat and corn fields close. All the people retire before us and desolation is behind. To realize what war is, one should follow our tracks."

Although the Confederate Army fought Sherman's men at every turn, the Confederates were forced to abandon Atlanta, Georgia, on September 1. In mid-November, Sherman's army set out for Savannah as Lincoln was elected for his second term as president. Before leaving Atlanta, Sherman's men set fire to the city, burning most of it to the ground. Sherman's army arrived in Savannah on December 10. Along the way they blew up bridges, wrecked rail lines, burned farms and fields, and killed whoever opposed them. By the time Sherman reached Savannah, his army had left a path of destruction across Georgia 60 miles wide and 300 miles long. This dealt the South a horrible blow. Sherman's March was remembered by Southerners with bitterness for many years afterwards.

Sherman's march to the sea.

Reconstruction

Lincoln was assassinated on April 14, 1865, five days after the Civil War ended. Lincoln's firm leadership would be missed by a nation reeling under the destruction of war. Congress came up with a plan called Reconstruction to help the South. Congress divided the South into five parts. A Union general took charge of each part until the states had written a constitution.

Congress passed the Fifteenth Amendment to the Constitution giving blacks the right to vote. Congress passed many laws in the early 1870's granting full rights to blacks. The Civil Rights Act of 1875 made it illegal to keep blacks out of theaters, hotels, railroads, and other public places.

For the next two years, blacks in the South faced harsh discrimination. The struggle for equality continues to this day.

Lincoln assassinated in Ford's Theater by John Wilkes Booth.

INDEX

ABOLITIONISTS 22-23, 24, 38
ALAMO 6, 7
AMERICAN ANTI-SLAVERY SOCIETY 22, 23
ANTIETAM, MARYLAND 38
ASSOCIATED PRESS 13

BARTON, CLARA 41
BATTLE OF BULL RUN 35-36, 37, 38
BOWIE, JIM 6

CHRISTIANITY 18
CIVIL RIGHTS ACT 46
CIVIL WAR 21, 27, 28-45, 46
CONFEDERATE ARMY 27, 28, 29, 30, 32, 33, 34, 36, 37, 42, 43, 44
CROCKETT, DAVY 4, 5, 6

DAVIS, JEFFERSON 27
DOUGLAS, SENATOR SPEPHEN 25
DOUGLASS, FREDERICK 23

EMANCIPATION PROCLAMATION 38-39

FIFTEENTH ADMENDMENT 46
FORT SUMTER, SOUTH CAROLINA 27, 28
FORTEN, CHARLOTTE 41

GARRISON, WILLIAM LLOYD 22
GETTYSBURG, PENNSYLVANIA 42
GOODYEAR, CHARLES 13
GRANT, ULYSSES S. 42-44

HOUSTON, SAM 5, 6, 7, 8, 9

IRON 14

JACKSON, GENERAL THOMAS "STONEWALL" 30, 31, 36

KEARNY, COLONEL STEPHEN 11

LINCOLN, ABRAHAM 26, 27, 28, 29, 37, 38, 44, 46, 47
LEE, GENERAL ROBERT E. 28, 30, 37, 38, 42

MCCLELLEN, GENERAL GEORGE 37, 38
MEXICAN-AMERICAN WAR 8-12, 35
MORSE, SAMUEL 13

NUECES RIVER 8

PEAKE, MARY 41
PLANTATIONS 16, 18, 23
POLK, PRESIDENT JAMES 10

RAILROAD 12, 13
RIO GRANDE RIVER 7, 8, 10
RECONSTRUCTION 46
REPUBLICAN PARTY 25-26

SAN ANTONIO, TEXAS 6
SANTA ANNA, ANTONIO LOPEZ DE 4, 6, 7
SHERMAN, GENERAL WILLIAM T. 44-45
SLAVERY 4, 8, 15, 17-21, 22, 23, 24, 25, 26, 28, 38, 39
STOWE, HARRIET BEECHER 23-24

TAYLOR, SUSIE KING 41
TAYLOR, ZACHARY 10
TELEGRAPH 13
TEXAS 4-12
TRUTH, SOJOURNER 41
TUBMAN, HARRIET 20, 21, 41
TURNER, NAT 19
TURNER'S REBELLION 19

UNDERGROUND RAILROAD 20-21
UNCLE TOM'S CABIN 23-24
UNION ARMY 27, 28, 29, 30, 32, 34, 35, 36, 37, 42, 43, 44

VULCANIZED RUBBER 13